Outgrowing Vanilla

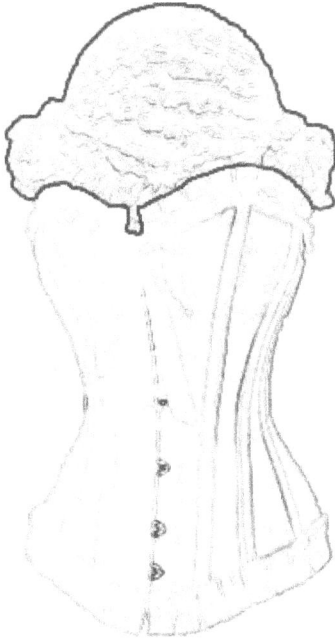

Discovering the Taboo Culture of Dominance and submission

by Karen Godson

Outgrowing Vanilla:
Discovering the Taboo Culture of Dominance and submission
By Karen Godson

Published by Riff Raff Publications
2011
riffraffpublications@gmail.com

ISBN: 0-9782516-5-2

This book is dedicated to Lucy, my beautiful wife who has encouraged me to follow my dream, and who has inspired me since the moment we met. A wave of love goes to my kids, who have grown up seeing their mother live life with openness and pride, and who have evolved into the most incredible mature human beings. I wish to also acknowledge the multitude of anonymous Dominants, submissives and those curious about the D/s Lifestyle, whose questions and interview answers are the heartbeat of this book.

TABLE OF CONTENTS

Introduction

This book is long overdue. Too many years have gone by in which "Dominance and submission" has been considered a taboo phrase to be whispered in the bedroom only. In some cases, not even the bedroom is considered a "safe" place. Within an otherwise secure relationship, one partner may be afraid to approach the other with the news that they are submissive and wish to relinquish control. This is especially true of men who are submissive yet fear being ridiculed by their wives or girlfriends if they reveal their true nature. They remain silent, and therefore their needs go unmet, often forced into suppression.

What is overlooked is that the accepted behaviours, beliefs and rules of this relationship type are merely carried forward from what were once the norms in society. It is a fact that in all human interactions there is a more Dominant and a more submissive participant, such as teacher/student, boss/employee, successful business people/people who struggle to stay afloat. It is the personal, intimate relationship dynamic of Dominant and submissive that is the focus of this book; the relationship between a dominant partner and their submissive mate.

Whether you are of the serving mindset, longing to help elevate your partner, or you are naturally the dominant figure in the relationship wanting to know how to officially take the helm, there is a safe place for you to express yourself. You are not a freak, nor are you a sinner. You are a human being who is aware of your position in society, or at least in intimate relationships.

It is important to understand some terminology before you begin your journey. For instance, a relationship that is based on the equality of the individuals and which is considered to be "Normal" in and out of the bedroom is called a **Vanilla** relationship. Typical "non-kinky" sex is called Vanilla sex.

Non-Vanilla aka "Kinky" Relationships

D/s (Dominance/submission): a mutually agreed upon power exchange between a naturally dominant person and a naturally submissive person. A Dominant, referred to as Domme if female and Dom if male, is the leader and decision maker in the relationship. The submissive for the most part has given over control of the finances and household decisions to the dominant partner. Often called Role Reversal in heterosexual relationships, the stereotypical submissive housewife is actually a dominant woman, and she takes on the role of the bread winning partner that has in the past been designated to men.

S/M (Sadism/Masochism): the relationship between a Sadist (one who derives pleasure from inflicting pain on others) and a Masochist (a person who derives pleasure from receiving pain). Note that NOT all Sadists are necessarily dominant; nor are all Masochists submissive.

M/s (Master/slave or Mistress/slave)   : an agreement of Voluntary Servitude and Ownership between Master and slave or Mistress and slave. It is not to be confused with S/M which stands for Sadism/Masochism. Although the worlds may sometimes intertwine, they are not interchangeable. Notice the use of a capital *M* for Master or Mistress, and a lower case *s* for slave. In S/M, both are capitalized. It is important to remember that a Dominant is not a Master or Mistress unless they own a collared slave.

BDSM is a creative acronym of the above mentioned terms with *B* for **Bondage** added for those who like to play with restraints and confinement. To understand the dynamics of Dominant/submissive and Sadist/Masochist and Mistress/slave relationships, one must recognize these differences between them.

More detailed descriptions of these alternative lifestyles are found in the Glossary section of this book.

Keeping it Simple

For the sake of fluid reading I will use terms throughout this book that reflect the typed protocol of the BDSM world. I will capitalize the first letter of words such as "Her" and "She", "I", "Me", "My", "Mine" , "Master", "Mistress", "Dom", "Domme" etc when referring to Myself or another Dominant person. I will likewise use lower case first letters in words like "he", "his", "she", "hers", "you", "yours", "submissive" when referring to a person with a submissive nature. Hence you will see a capital "Y" or "H" or "S" in the middle of a sentence, and a lower case at the beginning where a capital should be.

In almost all cases, I use a capital first letter when talking about a Person who is in the dominant role, and a lower case first letter for one in the submissive position. There is one exception; I use a capital D for dominant when it is being used as a noun, such as,

"A Dominant should come home to a waiting submissive".

When used as an adjective, the d is lowercase and the noun (proper name or pronoun) is capitalized. For example,

"A dominant Woman should come home to Her waiting submissive".

I will refer to males with a lower case first letter, and Females with an Upper case first letter. I do this because I am a dominant Woman, and I am writing from My perspective. It may not be the same perspective as yours, and I respect that. The beauty of being human is the ability to make choices and have opinions (until collared that is!).

In all cases where a specific gender is mentioned, that gender may be interchanged with the opposite sex to reflect the reader's own situation.

You Are Not a Freak!

The purpose of this book is to educate the newcomers and the curious about the hush-hush behaviours, rituals, rules and guilt free (notice I did not say "guilty") pleasures of these underground cultures. Many in society would call people in these lifestyles sinners, hedonists, abusers, narcissists, and more. Again, their perspective; in this case one which is founded on the doctrines of organized religion. Before major organized religions existed, people did not feel shame in wanting to be in control, or shame in desiring a lowly position in order to serve others. There was nothing wrong with knowing ones place, and living within it. After all, Nature says there has to be a leader. All others are followers; period.

People who are curious about D/s, or S/M, or M/s tend to feel as if they would be frowned upon or called freaks if their friends, family members or partner were to find out about their kinks. Busted in a locker room by his team mates, a guy may fib that he shaves his legs "for swimming", or a young woman joke to her friends that if her boyfriend complains about her new hair do, she'll gag him with her rolled up underwear. These admissions are usually shrouded in nervous laughter that is an attempt to disassociate the confessor from the confession. The fact is, these people are reaching out, hoping someone else will identify with them and they will no longer feel they are alone, abnormal or a freak. What this book is meant to do is blow away the taboos and allow people to stand up and say,

"I'm kinky and it's ok!"

Celebrate that you made it this far. It is only the beginning of a beautiful, magical journey! Open the door and step through...

1

Are you submissive?

In all (yes I said all) of Nature there must be opposites. To hot, there is cold. To darkness, there is light. To up, there is down. To dominant there is submissive.

Looking Up

Some fortunate people already know where they stand; which role they belong in when it comes to relationships. This chapter is meant to help those who feel they are destined to live as submissive to their Partner. If you are not positive that you are submissive, ask yourself these few simple questions for clarity:

- Do you imagine yourself looking up into your partner's eyes as you sit at Her feet, your arms wrapped around Her legs and your head in Her lap?

- When you hug, are your arms under Her arms, even if you are taller?

- What are your feelings around an exchange of control, or loss of power?

- Do you wish you could look away from the waitress when she arrives at your table, so that she must ask your Partner for your order?

- Are you having trouble in your relationships because you are expected to behave in an assertive way that is not you?

The world of dominance and submission is the world of Natural relationships. Every wolf pack has a leader; an Alpha wolf that is in charge of who eats and when, where the pack lives, who sleeps on which bed, who mates with whom, etc. Communal living without a chain of command spells chaos. Seagulls, for example live together without a solid social structure. Theirs is a life of ever changing power struggle. Sure, they hang out together bobbing on the waves and basking in the sun, but look what happens when there is a challenge, such as the distribution of scarce food resources. When the French Fry truck pulls to a stop at the boardwalk and opens its window, the gulls swoop in and go ballistic over one fry. Why? It is because there is no leader. No one has established their superiority and their right to eat first. The screeching is just the vocal part of the struggle for control. There is so much more going on in the subtle bobbing of heads and flapping of wings.

When there are challenges in your relationships, is there screeching? Is there also the subtle dance of who is going to take the Alpha role? Do you or your partner even know that this is what is happening? Sadly, you are not alone if you do not recognize the chaos. Most couples, or singles who wish to be in a relationship fail to see that they may be living in roles that do not suit their nature.

In the face of a challenge, some very masculine men just want to bow out gracefully and give the control to someone else. However, there is some unspoken assumption that they are going to look after things because they are men and "that is what men do". Somehow, society has allowed itself to believe that a submissive man is a weak man. This is simply not the case.

In Vanilla (commonly referred to as "normal", though that is under debate) relationships, partners may argue far more often than they would like, yet not understand why. It is because they are attempting to fit into holes that are a completely different fit than their personalities' "shape". But how does someone define their natural role? What should they look for in themselves, and what do they

watch for in a potential match? Is there a certain dress code? Perhaps
there a piece of jewelry that says "Dominant". As a matter of fact there is, but not all of Us own one!

Perhaps because I live this way 24-7, I do not feel the need to dress in a black leather corset and miniskirt, and parade around screaming that I am "a Domme". People who are submissive are just naturally drawn to Me. Some know why, and some do not.

Some dominant Women do choose to wear clothing that sets Them apart from the crowd, as a sort of calling card that announces that They are in charge. If these Dominants are single, you can bet They are scanning the horizon looking for someone whose eyes immediately avert upon contact with Theirs! If you want to be noticed as submissive by the Queen of your heart, then you must let Her see you looking at Her, and then let Her see you looking down right away, like a submissive wolf that has just been caught making eye contact with the Alpha wolf.

When someone is unsure of the other person's position, there could be miscommunication, misunderstandings and hurt feelings. However, if a submissive man could know for a fact that he has no decision making powers when in the presence of a certain Female, there would be no debate and therefore no stress. With submission there is a real sense of freedom; of relief and release.

But this chapter isn't about "them". It is about *you* and how this freedom would affect you. Of course, being new to the scene, you cannot know how it would truly feel to be in a Dominant/submissive relationship. you never will, either, unless you step outside of your comfort zone and start living as you were meant to live!

For those of you who are in a Vanilla relationship; now you must learn how to approach the subject of dominance and submission with your Partner without fear of rejection or ridicule. Just remember that to all Dominants there must be submission, and to all submissives there must be Someone who is willing to receive their gift of servitude. There is no giver if there is no Receiver of the gift. It is possible that your Lover is just waiting for you to surrender, so She can finally get on with steering the ship!

Now, where to start? I think you already have a pretty good idea, which is why you have this book in your hand. Start by learning. Accept your role, embrace it, and live it without shame!

The Need for Nurture

The need to be nurtured does not make you weak or infantile. It is innately human, and males who try to suppress that need are denying themselves something wonderful.

When things are not going well in life, a good cry sometimes helps. In many cases, a submissive man may not have a time and place where he can just let go, so his mind creates scenarios that it finds comfort in from past experiences. A kind hand on his cheek, or a lap to lay his head in as that hand strokes back his hair, are things his brain connects with feeling loved and nurtured. In some respects he is lucky; his mind acknowledges that he has a need, and it is showing him a solution. It tells him to seek a strong, confident Woman to comfort and protect him. Others may not know what the need, nor the solution is, and may find themselves in perpetual misery. Submissive men, feel better knowing that your needs are not only valid but are understood. As you fall asleep, imagine yourself nestled in the lap of a caring, gentle but authoritative Woman, Her arms shielding you so that you can at last let your guard down.

Honesty Is Everything

There is enormous power of attraction when the true nature of submissive meets the true nature of Dominant. The energy can be mistaken for love, or an exaggerated sense of *need* to serve if you are not careful. In the matter of one conversation you might go from meeting a Domme to feeling like the only way you can live is if you are allowed to be at Her feet. In normal circumstances, this would be considered extreme. However, because there are so many more submissives than there are Dommes, it is inevitable that there be some feeling of desperation to be the one She favours.

Use extreme caution and do not jump the gun. It is very important that you do not commit to serving a Mistress full time if you are not truly ready for all that entails. Personally, I am careful when speaking with new people who say they wish to be dominated by Me. I make sure they realize ALL of the implications of that. Some go as far as to say they live to serve. Sometimes I may test them to see how submissive they really are. When I ask them a question that involves their opinion, I can tell if serving is their first thought. A true submissive person will answer with "Your opinion is the only one that matters". A somewhat submissive person will reply, "It is my humble opinion that..." Someone who is just looking for Domme/sub role play, or who is not truly submissive might answer "Well, I think that..." Test complete.

As a submissive you owe it to your future Domme to know already if you are cut out for the lifestyle. It is important that you know without a doubt that this is meant for you, before you allow your Goddess to think you are "out" when you are not. If you think you can serve Her 24/7 in public as well as in private, realize that would mean telling your kids, friends, and your parents about your choice. You have as much responsibility to be honest up front about your availability as She does to tell you that She has other subs (submissives). Perhaps you are able to commit to just evenings, but your days are filled with full time work. Tell Her that, so She can decide if that is enough for Her to have your complete devotion from

6 pm until dawn each day. If you have truly thought it through and are ready to embrace your submission, to drop everything and live for the happiness of your One, then bless you and good luck. It is a beautiful world to be in.

Self-training

After years of struggling in relationships where you felt grossly misunderstood, you have finally come to the realization that you are probably submissive. you are the yin to the Dominants' Yang. you live to be in the service of Another, and long for the safety and security of Her rule. One thing scares the hell out of you, though; that first step into the dark and delicious world of Dominance and submission. It can be extremely intimidating for a new submissive; the fear of immediate rejection, being over-zealous or offending a Domme and pushing Her away.

There is no need to feel intimidated if you do your homework ahead of time. If you are serious about being the best submissive partner that you can be, then a little work and practice will be no sacrifice at all.

Start with this: **PAY ATTENTION !**

One thing that is extremely frustrating for a Dominant is receiving emails or online messages that clearly show a complete lack of obedience. We can tell an inexperienced submissive from a mile away; sometimes in just one or two words. This is because in some cases, one or two words are all the sub has sent in the message! FYI; there are about 500 submissives per Dominant in any given online community. If you want to be noticed, you must SELL yourself. I don't mean pimp yourself out. I mean talk volumes about what you can do for HER...not what kinky things you have done in the past. If She wants to know, She will ask.

Personally, messages like "nice hair", or "how r u?" do not get a reply from Me. I can guarantee that if you have sent a message like this to Me or any other Domme, it was deleted unread. Don't sit there scratching your head, wondering why. Go back and read Her profile! If it says "Do not message Me with one liners", "DO use proper grammar and spelling. I will not respond to text speak." and you fail to comply with Her rules, how can She be sure that you will follow Her instructions at home? Right. She can't. So before you even think about approaching a dominant Woman for the first time, or confessing your nature to your current Partner, you had better learn a few things. There are tips that you will need in order to save yourself from the slaughter that awaits you if you piss the wrong Domme off! There are certain rules you must follow. Just as in nature, there are right and wrong ways for you to present yourself to a Dominant "for consideration".

Before you approach your partner or potential Domme and tell Her of your desire to give Her control, you should do some preparation so that you can present to Her the best package possible. Consider doing some self training in confinement, silence, perfect cleanliness of self and household, and even meditation (putting your intentions out to the Universe) for the purposes of engraining the submissive or slave mindset.

Protocol When Typing

Because society relies so heavily on electronic communications these days, it is important for newcomers to the D/s and BDSM worlds to learn how to approach any Dominant online. A general "rule of thumb" for online communication helps remove uncertainty. When addressing a dominant Woman for the first time through text, chat, email, web site messaging or plain old fashioned name and number on a napkin, a submissive must make it obvious that he is aware of Her superior position by capitalizing Her name and all personal pronouns referring to Her.

For complete details, go back to Introduction: Keeping It Simple.

Here is one example; I received a message from a slave-hopeful (meaning he wanted me to own him), complimenting Me on My smile and wishing Me a lovely day. He neglected to follow the rules of protocol that My profile had clearly laid out. I responded with a reprimand but with gentle guidance explaining how he should have typed the message.

The slave-hopeful then replied to My correction, thanking Me for My lesson on using *capitals* to address Dominants. Ironically, he did not use capitals in his thank You message either. I re-wrote the original message for him in italics, replacing each lower case "y" he had typed with an Upper case RED one, and sent back this reply.

"you are welcome. However you did not use capitals this time either. Try again. It has to become habit. EVERY time you type to a Domme, you must use a capital when referring to Her. This is how you should have typed to Me.

"Hello Ma'am. What a beautiful smile You have, and Your eyes are simply sparkling. I hope You have a great day.

At Your service,

bobby"

As Dominant, it is My responsibility to correct his mistakes so that he may learn. As submissive, it is his job to not make any!

In another example, a female slave candidates wrote Me the following message;

"slave looks forward to speaking with Miss K at her convenience."

Notice that this slave-hopeful has made the same error in her message as the male above made. In the message, she said, "slave looks forward to speaking with Miss K at her convenience."

If this potential slave was referring to Me as "her", then she failed to adhere to the rule of capitalizing all pronouns referring to Dominants, such as "She", 'You", "Her" etc. If the slave was referring to herself as "her", then she is wrong to assume that chat will be at her convenience, and not Mine. It is a lose/lose message and it was corrected promptly.

Sound totally confusing? No need for it to be. Just remember that you, as submissive, would be looking UP at your Partner from your knees, so you use UPPER case for Her. As submissive, you are looked down at (not down upon!) by your Dominant and therefore are designated the *lower* case first letter. It's simple, and it shows automatic respect for the Dominant that other potential partners may lack. It is important that you strive for perfection in yourself, so that Others see your value. On just one BDSM personals web site alone, I have scores of subs and slaves of all genders asking if they can serve Me. Out of many "candidates", a Domme may only be looking for one. Who will it be; one of them, or *you*?

Locked, Not Loaded

While you are striving to make yourself worthy, this is a perfect opportunity for you to learn self control and practice chastity. your arousal at the thought of your Goddess is flattering but non-productive, especially if you are serious about your submission. Most boys cannot control their urges like Women can. Dominant Women understand that and use it to enslave you, but the ironic thing is, you come willingly led by your libido.

Sadly, oversexed submissives can grow tiresome to the point where the Dominant loses interest in the person themselves. Before you dig your own hole, do a self-check to see how much of your need to be dominated is sex-linked. Is it all about the orgasm when you are restrained, or is it about pleasing your Lover? Are you prone to saying or doing stupid things because you acted with lust and did not think first?

you can teach yourself to meditate through your desires, and tell your arousal that it is not welcome. Rise above (no pun intended, boys) it and take pride in knowing that you CAN keep it at bay. If you were the submissive in a D/s relationship, arousal restrictions, orgasm control and even the wearing of a locked chastity device might be imposed on you so now is a good time to start mastering those skills of self-denial while it is still *your* idea!

To begin, you will need to come up with a trigger that helps you to become aroused. Be it a visual fantasy, a smell, a song or other stimulus, try to take advantage of its power and let yourself go with it. Allow yourself to become aroused, and notice how easily you can get a physical reaction to a mental or emotional stimulus.

Now, as you are feeling this wonderful mental pleasure, you naturally want to follow it with physical pleasure and then release. This is the part that requires your full commitment to pleasing your partner. As you begin to fight internally with yourself, trying to justify WHY it wouldn't hurt anything or anyone for you to do it just this one time, your inner conflict's winner is determined by your conviction and dedication to your end goal. What if your Partner asks you to delay orgasm so that you can please her longer, or She directs you to pleasure her orally, but has no intention of rewarding you with reciprocation because you failed to complete your day's chores? Isn't it better to know ahead of time how to control your urges, so that you can please Her, and be allowed the beautiful orgasm that is given by Her permission, or ordered at Her direction?

In order to deny yourself self-pleasure, you first need to learn to control the initial mental arousal. Stopping the arousal in its tracks takes away the need for physical release because you have not allowed the sexual pressure to build in the first place.

As your mind begins to form the fantasy that leads to physical sensations of arousal, you must direct the thoughts to something else. Take your imagination by the hand and say "Yes, She is amazing and, Oh my God, She makes me want to..." but then substitute the rest of that typical "horn dog" ending to your sentence with "... do ALL I can to please Her."

Tell your mind that pleasuring yourself is stealing from your Beloved, and that is hurting Her. Do you really want to hurt the One Whose feet you long to massage and kiss? No. Then train yourself to focus your energy on other things so that when She does call you to Please Her, you are 100% Hers.

First, try going for two days without masturbation or orgasm, then work up to four days, then a week. You will be surprised that you can actually live without it! And the less you focus on pleasing your own body, the more you can devote to satisfying your Beloved.

Silence is Golden

In the presence of a Dominant, a submissive should be demure, polite, quiet and agreeable. A slave on the other hand should be silent until asked to speak. Some Dommes may like their slaves to sing as they work, or to talk to Them, and some may have a "Don't speak until spoken to" rule. In either case, it would benefit you to teach your mouth to stay shut. Use time when no one is around to practice your vow of silence, so nobody wonders why you are being rude and ignoring them. If you don't have to answer the phone, don't. Spend as long as you can; all day and night if possible not uttering a sound of any kind. No humming, throat clearing, or moaning is allowed. If you can stay completely silent for at least 8 hours, you have a huge advantage over other submissives who have not yet taken this into consideration.

Staying in your Place

Yes, it is true that boys, if left to their own devices would make a complete mess of their lives! It is Our job as Dominant Women to keep you in your place, and keep your minds focused and clear.

When someone tells Me he wants to serve a Domme, but he is very assertive and dominant at work, it makes Me wonder if his dominant nature might one day bring trouble. Are you able to say for a fact that once you are in submissive role at home, you would never dream of trying to lead? Most Dommes would certainly need to be assured of that before taking on the risk of a submissive that talks back or voices strong opinions. A submissive partner who tries to direct or control the relationship even in the most subtle or passive aggressive ways, or who speaks against his or her Dominant is said to be "topping from the bottom". This is something Dommes will not tolerate. Remember, when a Domme wants your opinion, She'll give it to you.

So how do you teach your ego to stay where it belongs? you develop mantras, meditations so to speak, that repeat over and over again what your intentions are. The Universe will pick up your vibrations and draw what you seek to you, if you are specific and sure. If you waiver in your intentions (eg "I want to be completely controlled... *as long as I can keep my job*") then your result will not be what you had hoped for. Instead, set an intention or affirmation daily that says "I am truly submissive. I am like a humble, quiet Geisha in all that I do".

Confinement

Sometimes rather than use corporal punishment to reprimand a slave or submissive, a Domme might choose to employ confinement. She may decide to put the offender in a closet, and deny him any form of stimulation for a pre-determined length of time. If you became nervous or anxious just reading that sentence, and think you might wig out or have a panic attack if locked in a closet, then you had better desensitize yourself now! I suggest starting by putting in ear plugs and wearing a blind fold and sitting in the smallest room or biggest closet you have. MAKE SURE it is one that can be opened from inside, since most likely you will be doing this when alone the first time. Close the door and sit or stand for at least ten minutes before you let yourself out. The next time you do it, stretch the time to twenty minutes, and then thirty. Some Dommes have been known to confine their slaves for days at a time, bringing them only food and water, and allowing them a toilet to use. Now you must understand as the reader of this for possibly the first time, that there are those who seek out specifically Dominants who will reduce them to objects. They specify in their online profiles that this is something they crave, long for, and beg for. As odd as it may seem to want to have all of your freedom taken away, it is a desire that is shared by thousands and thousands of people worldwide. Don't believe Me? Go online and search "BDSM dating" and see for yourself what some of the profiles are saying!

Ok now back to you. How badly do you want to please your partner, or impress a Dominant that you have not yet met? Are you willing to invest a little time and work in yourself? Great! Then get to it!

Dress Up Doll

Right now, your heart is probably racing and you are deathly afraid that someone is going to catch you reading this. So far, everything has been internalized; your ideas and thoughts have been your own so you had no way of being discovered. you were safe.

This is different. Putting on a pair of panty hose is not in your head. It is out there, for anyone to see who happens to walk in on you.

you know something deep inside, though. In a way you wish someone WOULD notice, so you could finally let out your breath and explore your desires. Call it a kink, or a fetish, or a sexual fantasy.

Who cares? Just buy that pair of silky stockings and start living your life with some freedom. Remember at the beginning of the book that I said "Gulit-Free, not Guilty, pleasures"? Let that soak in for a while, and start thinking along those lines. There is NOTHING WRONG with you. Period. You are allowed to wear whatever you want...until your Mistress tells you otherwise, that is!

It is not that simple is it? For some it is. A few of you are already walking into the lingerie shop, thinking,

"I wonder what cup size I am!"

All you were waiting for was a green light.

But what if you are not one of those people? Perhaps you are someone who just cannot bring yourself to follow your desire to dress in ladies clothes unless ordered to so by Someone else. It is what you would see as self-indulgent and you are the furthest thing from that. Instead, you live in silent longing, hoping to one day meet Someone who has a fetish for imposing cross-dressing on their partners. You don't have to long, nor do you have to wait. you can take steps to please your Goddess before you even meet Her. Learn how to start dressing so that when you are ready to "come out", you will have experience, and own a wardrobe that pleases Her.

Back to the task; if you are from the first group, you are already in the car, on the way home to try on your three piece satin teddy ensemble, despite being sent to the store for *one simple pair of pantyhose*. For advice on how to follow instructions, refer to the section called OBEDIENCE TRAINING.

If you are from the second group who needs to be ordered to cross dress because you fell that it is not your place to make that decision, then consider yourself told. I am giving you direct instructions to dress, as you have been longing to do. you might be in a domestic situation, making it difficult to find time alone in any capacity that allows you to feel safe trying on women's underwear. No doubt you are afraid that your girlfriend or wife will walk in and catch you and then you'd be outing yourself before you have even finished reading this book. Good! Then you can finally get on with exploring, and maybe even finish reading together.

Lack of privacy is a valid concern but is not a reason to remain inactive. It can not become an excuse for denying your own happiness. Go to the Dollar Store, buy a $1 pair of pantyhose, take them to a gas station and try them on in the washroom. Don't balk at My instructions. You are safe with Me, I promise. Just do as you are told now, and later it will be second nature to pull on a nice pair of stockings when your Mistress tells you to get dressed for a special occasion.

Roll Out the Hose

Putting on a pair of stockings or pantyhose for the first time can be very challenging. Too much pull could tear the delicate fabric, causing a run that only gets bigger as you move. To avoid runs, first make sure your hands are soft, free of hang nails and calluses. Ah, great news for the Metrosexuals; an excuse to get a manicure.

Now, roll the top of the panties portion up like you are rolling a sock to put on. Continue rolling the material into your hand, and begin to gather up one of the legs. Keep rolling until the toe portion is in your hand. Carefully put one foot into the toe of the pantyhose, and slowly unroll them as you work your way back up from foot to thigh, taking care not to stretch the nylon too taut or poke your nails through it. Once you have reached your groin, repeat the same with the other leg, rolling the material up on itself towards the toe and then unrolling as you bring it up it to your hip. Pull the panties part on just as you would a pair of underwear.

Look in the mirror. There, doesn't that feel amazing? The material is like a second skin, only it is hairless and silky, so unlike your own. The constricting feeling reminds you that you are under Someone else's control, wearing a kind of body confinement because I, your "Mistress for now", told you to. I turned you into My plaything.

But wait. Barbie doesn't have that bulge in front. you'll need to get that thing out of the way if you want to appear, as well as feel feminine. I can help with that too. Consider this your introduction to CBT. What is CBT you wonder? you can read more on that later. For now, see the Glossary quickly for CBT, then come back here and finish what I told you!

Good boy. Now, pull your member back between your legs; up and back towards your tailbone, and then close your butt cheeks to hold it there. Don't be a sissy. I said PULL! Now, look in the mirror again. See that? Isn't that amazing? Feel that smooth front; that mound of flesh that feels so feminine. For a few minutes, you are slave girl, free of all rights and decision making responsibilities. you are My personal Dress Up Doll; My pantyhose-clad puppet. How does that feel?

Oh, no you don't! Get your hands out of there, boy. Do you have to read "Locked, not Loaded" again?

Not only are the pantyhose constricting in a physical way, but they have an emotional fit. They give you a feeling like you are Mine because I imposed them on you; My will pressing against yours, and against your skin, holding you bound until I give you permission to take them off. Now, imagine how amazing that could feel if the Person you love gave this gift to you. Why not allow yourself to be ready for that when it comes. Show Her that you have taken steps to be good at dressing so that when She tells you to "go get prettied up", you can show Her that you know exactly what She wants!

Corporal or Mental Punishment:

Pain or Shame

As touched on in the book's Introduction, not everyone who is submissive is a masochist. Wanting to feel the power of Another controlling one's life is very different than deriving physical pleasure from receiving pain. Sometimes they go hand in hand, and sometimes they don't. Make no mistake though; one does not have to feel a whip's lashes to know Mistress' wrath!

When it does come down to physical pain for punishment, I have been asked what I like to see in male subs vs female subs, and whether there is a difference in the way I treat them. My answer is, in part, that I tend to be a little less patient and a little less tolerant with males who misbehave. I am a bit more forgiving with girls. Aside from that, if the submissive has a high pain tolerance and I am in a particularly deviant mood, I may wish to push the limits a little regardless of the slave's gender. A masochistic submissive knows the consequences of doing wrong, and is ready for the punishment. Some feel that a having higher pain tolerance makes them more valuable to their Partner, and so they strive to increase their pain limits. If you need more pain to feel fulfilled or redeemed, and your Partner is willing to provide it, where is the harm? This is what society has yet to embrace, and what I hope this book will be instrumental in changing. Many years ago it was common practice for devout religious people to punish themselves or go to a Monastery and ask the Abbot to mete out a number of lashes in accordance with their sins. If the person seeking redemption or a Spiritual connection is asking to have physical pain inflicted on them, it is not for others to condemn them for it.

Often forgotten is a facet of pain that is completely emotional and entirely non-physical in nature. Some non-physical pain such as the fear of abandonment, or the anguish in knowing you have disappointed the One you worship, can be agonizing. Imagine being shut in a dark room, not being allowed to see or touch or smell Her, until She comes to let you out.

Arousing perhaps, but knowing that you truly pissed Her off and the reason you are in there is because She can't stand the sight of you…that hurts.

In one of My online profiles I talk about kneeling and corner time, dark closets and waiting on My words. Emotionally, these concepts seem to resonate with many submissives. One man said they spoke to him very deeply, yet intellectually, he said, this kind of life seemed unrealistic. Some may doubt that it is truly sustainable, being captive and oppressed, and wonder if someone in that life really would still feel the same after a week, a month, a year. However, the point is to not feel the same; rather, to let it change you and envelope you like a security blanket.

2

Are You Dominant?

Accepting the Gift and Taking Control

Your partner has come to You and said that he has feelings of wanting to hand over control to You. You realize that You have always felt You should be the leader, but friends and family just would not have understood, so You remained in Your assumed role. Still, what can it hurt to look into the workings of a Dominant's role, just to see what it would be like?

Dominants have a different need. Theirs is to be in control of their Own lives, and to guide, teach and shape the people in it. Not all Dominants are stern and sadistic. Many are nurturers, with a strong need to assume responsibility for their partner's overall care. These dominant Women may not like to be held, but they may very much enjoy the act of doing the holding, smoothing their partner's hair and being the maternal (or in male cases Paternal) figure. As a Nurturer, I prefer to comfort, soothe emotional hurts and "kiss it better". This is not the same as age play. I do not find sexual pleasure in being seen as a Mother. Rather, it is being a Female Authority figure with the power to heal pain, as well as mete it out in the form of punishment, that I love.

There are degrees of submission. The depth to which you'd expect you're your partner to give in or submit to you may vary with your own tastes. Some people are quite assertive in the day to day relationship dynamic, but in the bedroom they tend to not initiate. They prefer instead to defer to their partner to take the lead. This is a bedroom submissive. 24-7 submissives are people who are submissive in all aspects of the relationship, but who do have some input in decision making. The most submissive personality is the slave. A slave is a special person who has the desire and courage to give over COMPLETE (and yes I mean that literally) control of their lives to their partner. They want to be led in all aspects of their lives, from what to wear, to who to associate with, to what they are allowed to eat and when. A slave is someone who offers himself or herself freely, and with complete trust.

After a long day at work, I come in the door and expect to be pampered from the moment it closes behind Me. My slave girl should be ready to spring into action the second I get home. How does she know that I expect a hot tea on a cold night and a cold beer on a warm one? her training tells her. This is where My job and Yours as a trainer is most important. In order for Your slave or submissive to understand exactly what You want, You must teach him. To obey well, he must have strict guidelines that dictate his behavior around and away from You, his Dominant. He needs a set of principles that leaves no doubt about what is expected and acceptable. This way the slave not only behaves as required but keeps focus and learns to anticipate his Dominant's needs and wants. Furthermore it keeps the boy in line as he knows that any deviation from the rules will result in immediate discipline being taken.

Your man should make sure first that he understands what is expected, to avoid annoying You. Whether it is a special dish, a glass of wine or any other treat, it should be ready for You. Your bath should be ready for You, and whatever else pleases You. Your man should be at your beck and call, ready and focused on You.

Paving the Way

In order to facilitate this amount of attention being placed on You, You must initially take away any distractions that could steal his concentration. Perhaps You could take away his cell phone when he is in Your presence, so that no one can call and convince him that their need is more urgent than Yours.

Forbid him to watch television or play video games while You are home. This will allow his mind to be clear and free of other influences. his only thought should be,

"What can i do for Mistress, so that She is happy?"

Another great way to assure his full attention on a more permanent basis is to send him to a dark room or closet and leave him alone for an hour. Do this as soon as he wakes up one morning, so his bladder is full and he is hungry. Do not let him get dressed first, and if he is wearing pj's, have him take them off before going into the closet. Remove anything from the closet that he could use as covering. Turn off the light and close the door. DO NOT LEAVE THE HOUSE. Stay close to the room, but Let him hear You move about. Make Yourself a tea, call Your friends. Let him realize that You are completely ok without him, but that he is helpless without You. Soon he will understand that his entire being should be working towards Your ultimate happiness, so that You allow him to continue being in Your presence. You are after all a Goddess, and You have chosen to let him worship You.

Obedience Training:

Behaviour Modification

Obedience training entails unlearning old habits and learning new ones. It is a matter of putting positive reinforcement in the right places, and punishment also where it is warranted.

When first training a submissive or slave, it is important to be clear about Your expectations, so he doesn't accidentally displease You. Failure to give him proper knowledge of the rules is like setting him up to make mistakes. Why not instead show him the right way to please You? After all, as is his only desire in life is to see You happy, You will be fulfilling his needs as well as your own.

Acknowledging the Good Deeds

As a Dominant, it is your job to teach your submissive partner what it is You expect of him. It is up to you to reward good behaviour so that he understands that he has pleased You. Once he realizes that what he did was correct and that it made You happy, he will of course want to repeat that behaviour. However, if what he does is right and you never reward him, or even tell him he did a good job, how will he know that You are pleased? How will he know to repeat the desired behaviour? He won't. This could lead to frustration on Your part, and hurt feelings on his. For example, if You tell him that doing dishes is now on his chore list, but never give feedback on how well he does them, then how will he know if his cleanliness standard is up to Yours? And weeks into the future, if You find a spot on one knife, and then another, and realized they are all spotty, and had been all along, how could You suddenly be angry and expect him to have known You were not ok with spotty knives? So it is necessary whether training a dog or a slave, to reward good behaviour with POSITIVE REINFORCEMENT. This can be a pat on the head and a smile, or an edible treat, or a play session. Anything you do that is positive and is given directly after good behaviour will help to engrain that behaviour in the subject's mind.

Conversely, if you want to discourage bad behaviour, you must either withdraw something positive such as banning a favourite food, or dole out some form of discipline. Discipline or punishment does not necessarily have to be physical. Banishing him from the room and from your sight is very painful to a submissive partner. Being told that You can't stand being in the same room with him will certainly make him remember the terrible thing he did, and he will NEVER want to repeat that behaviour. This is NEGATIVE REINFORCEMENT.

A good animal trainer will tell you that learning cannot occur when there is no consequence to an action. If you tell your dog to sit, and he eventually does because it is a natural submissive posture, you reward him for sitting. You toss him a yummy treat, or lavish him with verbal and physical praise. You tell him that he did a good job, and then you RELEASE HIM from the sit, so he can recognize that the exercise is over. You let him walk away, or get up and play. This is important to the learning curve.

If you watch him sit, and then walk away and forget about him, he will not know that he did something right, and will get up and follow you, wagging his tail. If you then yell at him for not sitting, you are reprimanding him for a mistake he has no clue he made.

When You have demonstrated to your submissive partner or Your slave how You expect Your dishes to be done, then stand back and watch him do them himself. Give feedback on the finished job. If it is not good enough, demonstrate again. If You are satisfied, then praise him, reward him and let him know he is finished with dishes for the day. On an ongoing basis, check the dishes in the cupboard for spots if You do not like spots. It is up to You to maintain Quality control. If You see spots one day, call his attention to it, and do not accept any excuses. Simply tell him to rewash the dish. Tell him if it happens again, he will rewash ALL the dishes You own. If it happens a third time, the consequences will be less pleasant. I guarantee that unless he is a masochist or a brat (not a good trait to have in a sub or slave) then he will do a better job next time!

3

submissive or slave

As mentioned in the previous chapter, there are varying degrees of submission. Then there is voluntary slavery. Though a slave is the most submissive personality of all, a submissive person is not necessarily a slave. In order to know where your partner is willing to go in the relationship with regard to serving you or submitting to you, you must first establish their level of submission. Again using the example of the female in the relationship being Dominant, I will refer to submissives and slaves as "he".

In the Mistress/slave relationship, there is no negotiation. A slave willingly, knowingly signs his life over to his Owner, to do with him as She pleases. This is not bedroom-only role play. A slave is a slave is 24-7, with no rights other than those given graciously by Mistress. That is correct. I said NO RIGHTS. This is a person who has chosen to give over their entire right to have rights of any kind to another person. they are asking for their Dominant (referred to as Mistress once the slave is owned) to take over guardianship of their lives, financially, emotionally, physically, mentally and spiritually. When a slave has agreed to let Her control ALL aspects of his life, he removes words like "no" and "can't" from his vocabulary. he is aware that any and all decisions are Hers, and are final. he agrees to any form of training, confinement or punishment, physical, mental and emotional that She sees fit to deliver. A slave is not an extreme submissive. he is property, to be Owned, used, traded, sold, leased out or locked up at his Owner's whim. Some Owners will go as far as to refer to Their slave as "it".

In the Domme/sub relationship, the submissive has the option to submit to or decline commands doled out by his Domme. She and Her sub discuss their individual and mutual interests and limits. The Domme agrees to respect the sub's limits, and not force him to do anything that he is not comfortable doing. She may ask him to try harder each time She challenges him, but at all times there is the option to use a "safe word" and stop the activity. A slave does not have this right.

The Good s.a.m.?

Being the Owner or dominant Partner of a s.a.m. aka "smart ass masochist" is not fun, despite the s.a.m.'s insistence that their behaviour is playful and whimsical. Keeping these imps under control is exhausting, mentally and emotionally.

My first reaction to a s.a.m.'s behavior is this: somehow he has learned that he can get more in the way of attention from his Domme when he does something that pisses Her off. Being masochistic, he derives pleasure from pain. his smart-mouthed remarks and bad behaviours are meant to draw as much attention to himself as possible. Though the attention is negative, to a masochist, it is bliss. When there are other people besides his Mistress present, he may go out of his way to misbehave in front of everybody, knowing that he will be punished later. Therefore, his focus is not on pleasing his Domme, but on his own future gains. This alone must be corrected. How, then, does a Dominant discipline such a wayward sub without the punishment becoming a reward?

Simply put, he will have to be re-trained in a way that does not involve pain stimulus. his mind should be on one thing only, and that is pleasing his Mistress. The cocky, bratty, disobedient masochist must be taken back to his original status, and be reminded that he was ALLOWED to be with his Goddess, by Her grace alone. Anything that takes his mind away from serving Her is a distraction, and should be withheld until he is back in focus, eyes and mind set on his Domme. This may mean the withholding of his cell phone, TV, video games, Sunday golf and Monday Night football, or worse, banishment from Her presence.

Over the years I have discovered that there is another type of s.a.m. whose sassy remarks and broken rules are not meant to make his Mistress angry, though inadvertently it happens, and he probably IS quite sorry afterward. This one is not so much a "smart ass masochists" as he is a "smart ass submissive/slave". I have named this type "s.a.s." The issue the s.a.s. has is that he has low self-esteem, or is insecure in the relationship. he is not content when he is not the center of attention amongst a group of people, with all of them laughing at his jokes, patting him on the back. he often will misbehave at a party, speaking out and drawing others' attention to himself. he needs to feel liked by the majority, forgetting that all he should need is his Domme's approval.

In order to know that what he is doing is unacceptable, the s.a.m. or s.a.s. must be made to feel his Mistress' displeasure, and be made aware that there are consequences to his poor judgment.

Troubleshooting: A Domme should ask Her s.a.m. or s.a.s. point blank what he feels he is missing in the relationship. It does no good to ask "Is something wrong?". What will result is a passionless "No, Ma'am. Everything is fine, Ma'am".

Instead of asking a yes or no question, giving him an easy out, She should command him to ARTICULATE to Her what he feels he gains from misbehaving. The Dominant should have him take five minutes to REALLY think about his answer and then give it to Her. Only then will She be able to redirect his behaviour to bring about positive results and restore his respect for Her Authority. The Domme is doing the right thing by disciplining Her submissive for his misbehavior. At the same time She does want the cycle of misbehaviour = punishment to stop so She needs something to shift in his thinking. he must look at himself and find out what he is doing to sabotage the relationship, and why. He must be made to realize that THIS WILL NOT CONTINUE. No ifs, ands or buts. The behavior stops now, or the relationship does. If he cannot see himself behaving any differently, then perhaps it is time he is released, so that his Mistress may be better served by someone whose heart and mind ARE in the right place.

"Leniency is a good trait to possess, provided it is used sparingly." K.G.

4

Ask Ma'am Landers

During the writing of this book, I was approached by numerous people with questions about the Lifestyle of Domination and submission. This is possibly because I have lived My life openly, and made no excuses for My submissives calling Me "Mistress" in public.

I posted a message on Collarme.com and Fetlife.com, telling members that I was writing a D/s advice/self-help book and was looking for questions for My Q&A section. The response was overwhelmingly positive as you will see below. There were too many questions to publish in one edition, but some of the most helpful ones are in this chapter.

Because I have lived so transparently, people have felt safe in speaking to Me; asking questions about My experiences and about their own curiosities. Some seemed almost ashamed or embarrassed to reveal their true nature but those who did are responsible for the Questions in this book. They all deserve respect and admiration for their courage. Ah, yes, and they each received a free copy of this book! Thanks to them, your unasked question might be addressed here.

Q&A with Mistress K

Q- What is it about dominance and submission that You find so appealing?

A- Dominance and submission are like all other polar opposites in Nature. They are both very necessary for the smooth running of all social relationships in the Animal and Human worlds. The boss to employee relationship is one of Dominance and submission, and because the rules are clearly laid out as to who is in charge, there is rarely any serious struggle. If there is conflict, it is usually because either both are Dominant or both are submissive, or it could be that one of them is being forced to live in the role that is not congruent with the way they naturally feel. A submissive person by nature would not make the best manager, because they would not want to be the one making the decisions. A dominant person who is not allowed to carry any authority at work will also be miserable.

So it is with domestic partnerships. If one is Dominant and one is submissive, then there is no need to argue. Certain tasks are understood to be the responsibility of the submissive, and others belong to the Dominant. The reason I love the D/s lifestyle is because it is living as Nature designed U/us, and not the way society has dictated that W/we live.

Q- Have You ever personally experienced being submissive or have You always had a dominant nature?

A- For 8 years I was unwittingly the submissive partner in a miserable marriage. I was too young and naive to understand that My dominant nature around the animals in My life could be also employed in My relationships. It wasn't until I was divorced and started opening My mind to learning about all aspects of relationships, sexuality and human interactions that I realized I was much more natural the Dominant role. I had one relationship in which I tried to be submissive because the relationship was failing. I thought it would help. After a few months of that nonsense, My partner confessed that she was submissive and that was why nothing was ever accomplished. she was waiting for Me to take control, but failed to convey that. I would have, gladly, had I known. Instead, I tried to give her the reins, to empower her because I thought that would make her happy. W/we all have much to learn at first, and I am glad to say that learning is ongoing.

To sum it up, I have always had a Dominant nature. I just haven't always known how to live naturally in My role. Thankfully, now I do.

Q- Are some girls just born to be submissives and slaves? i mean is it in their true natur e; who they really are and need to be?

A- Absolutely, yes. Though all females are superior to males, there needs to be a natural balance of female submission and Female Dominance. It is within everyone's true nature to be one or the other or in some cases a touch of both.

I believe that W/we are born to either lead or follow. How W/we live life determines whether or not W/we get to "become" that which W/we know W/we are.

It might confuse a Female Supremacist to hear that there are truly submissive females, but it should not. Nature is all about balance.

Q-What is the one specific kink or activity that exceeded your ex pectations (as t o sens ual/erotic satisfaction) when you first engaged in that activity, and why?

A- The first time I used My flogger, I felt a sense of total ownership of My life, and that of the person I was flogging. It made My entire Domme experience suddenly complete, and I felt at one with the Sadistic nature that I had been unknowingly suppressing for so long.

The rush of power was incredible, but not the kind that would send someone out to conquer the planet...just every man on it. I felt TRULY SUPERIOR and that was intensely erotic.

I used to think I was just a Dominant Woman, not interested in S/M at all. Then I decided that it was not right to say I didn't like something until I had at least given it a try. I bought a braided fake leather belt at a Thrift Store and took it apart to re-form it into My now favourite toy. That flogger opened doors for Me that I didn't know I wanted to go through. Now that I know what is on the other side, I can't imagine going back.

Q- Does your level of sadistic intensity vary, depending on whether the subject is male or female? You seem to prefer impact as a means of delivering pain, would that be a correct statement?

A- Yes, My level of intensity does vary with the slave's gender. As yet I have not explored My sadisitc side as much as I would like to. It has mainly been mental imagery with some practical "hands on". I do notice that when I imagine flogging a male, I can see Myself inflicting a little more pain than I would on a female.

I cannot see Myself being an extreme pain Mistress. I believe I prefer non impact methods such as pinching and nipple twisting. I find nipple clamps to look barbaric, yet find pleasure in using My bare fingers to do the same thing the clamps do.

Q- Why is it as a s ubmissive masochist, when i push and explore new things that seem   more scary....that, these new things beco me mor e norm al, and i crave t   o push a st   ep further each time. At what   point does one say, "That's scary", and stop?

A- As you push yourself past the most scary things, and come out unscathed on the other side, your brain recognizes that particular "enemy" as having been conquered. Much like the first time you go for a ride on a terrifying roller coaster; your mind is racing, heart pounding and your inner voice is saying "you are out of your mind! Run!" If you talk yourself out of the flight instinct, and stay to fight (ie go on the ride) then end up surviving the danger, your brain rewires itself to recognize that particular roller coaster as NOT a mortal danger. The next time won't be as scary, and after many rides, the thrill will be gone and you will be seeking out more terrifying rides.

Now, if you have been telling yourself that being hung by giant hooks through your skin is a HARD LIMIT, but have been fantasizing about it, chances are your brain is seeing it as not a death defying risk. Maybe then it is a Soft Limit, or conceivably a Dislike. Therefore you can slowly and more easily talk yourself into it. The self preservation instinct can be re-trained, or as W/we say in the Lifestyle, your limits can be pushed.

Regarding knowing when to say stop:

As long as you do your research and proceed SAFELY, your brain WILL stop you when there is no possible safe outcome. The key is to be sane, find out the facts before pushing a limit, and don't do ANYTHING with Someone you don't trust 100%. It is a matter of knowing when to use a safe word. My advice is to count to five after the first thought of "I wonder if I should stop this". If after the count to five, you still wonder, then the answer is yes. You have already gone five seconds past your limit, and that is wonderful. No need to be a stuntman and go for ten. Save that for next time. You know there will be one.

5

Short Stories

The Hard Way

By Karen Godson

josie's heart raced as she heard the keys clinking in the hall outside her door. It seemed like she had been in her room for just a few hours, but with the sound of the keys came the realization that she had in fact been confined for a full day.

There was no window in the room. It was dark and musty smelling, like an old tent that had not been aired out properly. Somewhere in the blackness, water drops slapped against the concrete floor. The water must have been dripping from quite a distance in order to be so loud. josie found hypnotic comfort in the sound. It helped her count off the minutes in this solitary cell, where her Mistress had chosen to keep her when her service was not required.

It must be required now, josie thought, as the clunk of the lock tumblers turning over snapped her to attention. she jumped up so quickly that her head spun. she must remember to take her time so she doesn't faint, and start to stand up sooner the next time she heard the keys approaching. If Mistress happened to open the door before slave was in full position, She would not be pleased. Mistress' displeasure meant another 24 hours in the dark for josie, with only the drips and the burning whip marks on her back for company.

Slipping toward the side wall as quickly and quietly as she could, josie spread her legs far apart and placed her hands up on the cold wall. Mistress required that josie be spread eagle, hands apart and ass presented every time She came to open the door. If She heard the chains grating across the floor as She was turning the key, it meant that josie had not been paying attention and she would be punished. josie was fully aware of this, and though the thought of the whip's lash made her pussy throb, she did not like feeling Mistress' disappointment in her. she made sure most of the time to be listening for Mistress' approach, for that could be at any time day or night.

The trouble with being in the cell was that night and day did not exist. For josie, there was sleep time, meal time, bathroom time and silence. Mistress could be listening outside at any given moment, and if josie made a sound, even of the chains around her ankles clanking together, Mistress's concentration might be disturbed. That was not allowed under any circumstances, as Mistress was a writer and needed quiet.

With her pussy aching and a lump in her throat, josie wondered whether she had been quiet enough. Would it be the whip, followed by another day in here, or would she be told that she was a good girl, and be allowed out to play?

Mistress pushed the door in, and stepped through silhouetted by the light bulb behind Her. She was dark and ominous like an approaching storm cloud, yet so heavenly; josie's Goddess. Mistress kept her here because She loved josie like Her treasured pet, and in order to be allowed to stay, josie needed training. she understood and embraced her training because it allowed her to be at the feet of her Queen. Simply the touch of Mistress' hand sent spasms of wanting into josie's body like bolts of electricity.

Now, standing as she should be, josie listened carefully for a sound from her beloved Captor. her nipples stood erect and her well-muscled back straight; a back marked with the evidence of each lesson learned the hard way.

Lessons like "Do not cum until Mistress has given permission." were harder to learn than some others. josie recalled how hard it was to control her orgasm the time that Mistress had her completely immobilized on the bed and was stroking her freshly shaved pussy with a feather. The tickling feather sent tingles through every nerve ending in josie's wet lips and she longed to be released from the flood inside.

Mistress had the most wonderful toys; a Violet Wand for electric shock play, and the most beautiful colored candles to drip hot wax onto josie's goose-bumped skin. Oh how josie loved to feel the burning wax as it landed on her hard nipples. It immediately formed a sealed dome that continued to burn for a few seconds, and then cool so that it hardened and pinched her nipple skin. It was an intense roller coaster of sensitivity that almost made her cum just thinking about it.

And there she went again, letting her mind wander until her body followed...

josie heard Mistress speak, and snapped very quickly out of her day dream. she heard the tail end of the sentence, and recognized the happy tone to mean that there would be no whip today. Mistress was pleased with her for being so quiet and was going to take her upstairs for a treat.

josie squealed like a joyful puppy, but stood perfectly still as Mistress unlocked the ankle restraints. josie felt naked without them. They were her physical reminders of her place as slave, and being without them was like suddenly being without a wedding ring.

A stern look from Mistress at the squeal made josie bite her tongue; literally. Mistress had told her that if she could not learn to be silent, she would have to actually bite her tongue until it bled. The taste of blood and the pain of a sore tongue for a few days were effective silencers, as was the glare from her Owner. josie was quiet and swallowed her blood tainted excitement.

In the now dim light of the room josie saw the leash clip coming toward her. she knew that she was going to be led by her collar; another reminder of her slave status. The collar stayed on at all times and was locked securely with a key that Mistress wore around Her own beautiful neck.

Once out in the hall, josie's eyes recoiled painfully at the brightness. she closed them tightly and walked on in faith that Mistress would not let her bump into anything. Mistress was sadistic, but not inhumane. Besides, if She was not actually inflicting the pain, it did not have the same effect. She was very aroused by seeing josie squirm under Her torture, but an accidentally stubbed toe, besides giving Her a chuckle, did nothing for Her.

Up the basement stairs josie obeyed her Queen's command to walk ahead, her pussy juices lubricating her upper thighs with each step as she neared the top.

her imagination was running away to all kinds of dark, delicious places when Mistress suddenly pulled her hair, hard. josie's head snapped back, and tears came to her eyes as she almost fell backward.

"girl! Pay attention. Don't fuck this up." She said in what was clearly a warning whisper.

With a shove through the doorway, Mistress let go of josie's hair, smoothed it out with a deliberate motion and then nodded toward the high backed chair that sat in the corner of the Living Room. josie was trained to kneel in front of the chair which was her Domina's throne, with her upturned hands resting on her thighs, and wait as Mistress gave her the next command. she dropped to her knees and assumed her position, eyes looking at the floor.

As her legs bent under her, josie could feel the pussy nectar spreading over her calves. It felt amazing. Her defined calf muscle had a ridge on it that sat just under josie's frustrated clit. When she lowered herself she put pressure on her clit, and then when she raised her ass back up slightly, it took the pressure off.

She did this often while Mistress prepared the room for play. It helped get her wet for her Goddess, so she considered it permissible. At least, she justified it that way.

This time, Mistress seemed to be taking an extra long time to get ready and josie was having a difficult time stopping the rocking. The anticipation made it almost unbearable, and josie felt herself nearing climax.

When she was sitting with her ass completely down on her calf, the wet pussy on wet leg feeling was intense. josie's lips ached to be parted. she pressed her pelvis forward and down. Her clit pulsed, begging to be rubbed hard and fast. Still, josie had to wait. All she could do was invisibly rock back and forth on her leg, and wait.

On the large wooden table, there were big steel D-rings that were bolted right through the solid wood legs. There were also rings in each corner of the table's top, and two in the center, one at each end. The table was an antique butcher's counter and was heavy as a Stonehenge slab, josie was sure. No matter how hard Mistress had fucked her, josie had never felt the table move.

At one end of the room was a rack that held all of the punishment and impact play devices, such as floggers, whips, paddles, riding crops, wooden spatulas and rubber bungee cords. Each of these had its own sting or bite, depending partly on the implement and partly, if not mostly Mistress' mood. When josie had been a good girl, these tools could become her best friends as they were part of foreplay in Mistress' loving hands. However, when Mistress was not happy with girl, any of these tools could bring a punishment to impress The Marquis de Sade himself.

Gazing like a deer in headlights at the toy rack, josie rocked back and forth so slightly that it was undetectable by anyone who might have been looking at her. she was so caught up in her waves of pleasure that she didn't hear herself moan.

As josie was blissfully riding her wet leg, she suddenly felt her Domina glaring at her. her heart dropped until she thought for sure she could feel it at the bottom of her stomach. she had been caught masturbating. With or without hands, self-pleasure was absolutely forbidden! josie had broken a very serious rule and was to be punished after all.

Mistress stomped over to josie and again grabbed her by the arm.

"What the fuck do you think you're doing?" she snarled. "Have I not told you that that pussy is Mine, and you are not to fucking touch it? Do I have to cut off your clit, you filthy slut?"

She pulled josie, teary eyed and shaking, to her feet and pushed her toward the table.

"This was supposed to be fun. I had a special day planned, but now you've just pissed Me off." she hissed as she threw Her slave onto the table top, face first.

josie's heart sunk even further when she saw the two Day Passes to the Leather Faire lying on the table under her nose. she knew enough to not struggle as her full, firm breasts pressed painfully into the wooden surface. she was in the wrong, and had no intention of making things worse! she spread her legs and arms apart like she was about to be frisked by the police, and waited as Mistress locked her ankle and wrist restraints. Feet locked to the legs of the table and hands to the top, to the farthest corners, josie was immobilized. It was her own fault, she knew, and she vowed to be quiet during her punishment, whatever it was going to be.

"Close your eyes" Mistress barked. josie did so without hesitation. She swallowed, hoping the gulping sound was not too loud.

"Now, once and for all I will explain to you Whose pussy that is, Whose body it is and Who has the right to fuck what part of it. Clear?"

josie blinked and looked away, careful not to meet Mistress' glare. she was not allowed to make a sound, and even an "Mmm hmmm" would have been an infraction of that rule.

josie stayed stock still in her restraints, her clit suddenly withdrawn and her sexual frustration left unsatisfied. she wanted to cry, but knew better. Mistress would only tell her that she brought this on herself by not being able to control her urges. josie used to believe that she couldn't help it, but Mistress was teaching her that indeed she could and would learn orgasm control. josie knew one thing; this was a lesson, she did not want to learn the hard way!

Behind her and out of sight, josie heard the drawer on the Sideboard slide open. It was the drawer where Mistress kept Big Bertha; a 9" strap-on that was as thick around as josie's wrist. It hurt when Mistress used Big Bertha, but josie liked the pain. It reminded her that she belonged to Mistress, and that she was a toy no different than those in the drawer to be used as Mistress saw fit.

Right now, Mistress was seeing fit to teach josie NOT to masturbate.

She walked to the foot of the table with Big Bertha strapped snugly to her pelvis, and promptly slapped josie as hard as She could with Her open hand, on josie's upturned ass cheek. josie, not expecting the shock, jumped a little and was immediately given another slap. To this one, she did not react.

"That's better", Mistress said as she stepped back to look at Her already welting hand marks. "Don't make Me bruise My beautiful slave-ass."

josie felt her pussy throb again. Mmmm, how she loved the sting of her Mistress' bare hand. It was never as painful as a whip or flogger, and it was always more intimate. It felt warm as the blood vessels beneath her skin reacted to the assault.

Mistress placed her hands on josie's hips and pulled her closer so that her tummy was barely on the table. josie was uncomfortable, stretching forward and reaching as her bound hands ached. Mistress reached Her hand down in front of josie, between her and the table, and felt for josie's hungry pussy. There it was, her hard, disappointed clit, begging to be rubbed still.

True to Her nature, Mistress dug Her nails into the soft flesh of josie's lips. She bent over the motionless slave girl, squeezed her nails in deeper and whispered,

"I could sew this shut if I chose to. Don't you forget it, girl."

She dug in again, knowing that josie wanted to jump away or whimper, but that she didn't dare. Mistress smiled unseen.

"And this", she said as she pinched the once again erect clit. "This is MINE. Do you fucking understand?"

josie blinked yes, but Mistress could not see her because her head was facing away. Mistress pinched again, hard. josie sniffed in a sharp breath, but did not budge.

"Good", Mistress said, backing away. "Let's not have to go over this again".

josie's pussy was so delicious. Mistress never really wanted to harm it, because She so loved to play with it, but there were times when She just had to tame the girl. josie knew this and accepted it gratefully.

When she felt the sharp pain of Big Bertha suddenly penetrating her without any warning, she did not move. She clenched her teeth, clasped her hands around the sides of the table, and curled her toes against the floor. But she did not make a sound.

As Mistress pounded Bertha in and out, over and over again, grabbing josie's hair with one hand and pinching her clit with the other, josie stayed silent.

"By the time I am done with you, you'll be too sore to wipe your ass".

Mistress reinforced Her message, twisting girl's clit until it felt like it was going to come off. It was bruised and swollen, but still she was not allowed to cum.

"Now", THRUST, "do", THRUST, "you", THRUST, "fucking", THRUST, "know", THRUST, "Whose", THRUST THRUST, "pussy", THRUST, "it is?" Mistress panted as She drove home Her message from behind.

The table moved.

josie was on the verge of cumming, the sweet fingernails of her Mistress imbedded in her clit hood. It was impossible to hold back any longer, yet she knew without question that she must not cum. Not yet, or ever again unless Mistress said so.

Finally, josie understood. All the times she had masturbated while Mistress had left her shut up in her cell, were times that she had stolen from Mistress. It was as bad as taking something form Mistress' purse, and josie, for the first time, felt deeply ashamed. How dare she even think to touch the Pussy that did not belong to her?

As josie came to the realization, Mistress could feel her body soften beneath Her. josie went almost limp with remorse, yet still did not move or make a peep. she stood perfectly still as Mistress crammed Bertha into HER pussy.

"Don't you dare fucking cum, do you understand Me?" She continued to ram Bertha inside josie's bruised hole, as the girl raised her hips in time with her Mistress' thrusting.

josie, in her bliss-swept mind, silently begged for more. She was thankful for the hard way, and wished she could scream out, "Oh yes! Fuck the bad girl right out of me!"

Mistress knew now that josie had finally grasped the rule of not pleasuring herself, and felt mercy on Her slave. She slowed Her thrusting and eased up on the clit torture, but did not take Her hand away. Methodically, she pulled Bertha out, and slipped it back in, as She bit josie's neck from behind like a dog holding its bitch down during mating. Slowly, in and out, side to side Mistress moved the huge strap-on, knowing that Her girl was verging on bursting.

"Ahhh, this is the sweetest torture of all", She thought. She felt Her helpless slave press back into the strap-on, trying to get it as deeply inside her as she could.

"Mmmm, now isn't that the way it should be? Don't I do it so much better than you do?" Mistress whispered as She slipped Big Bertha out of josie's battered pussy and without warning, buried it deep inside her ass.

The table moved again. And again.

josie buckled at the knees.

"Oh god, yes!", she answered silently. she wished she could speak, but did not want to disturb the heaven she was in. As Mistress forced her to surrender, josie went into another realm. The room spun, her clit pounded in time with her heart beat, and in the distance she heard her beloved Queen say,

"Now".

With a final thrust, Mistress and slave crashed together violently, their combined orgasms soaking legs, floor, and shackles. josie went limp against the table, and with grateful tears flowing down her cheeks and her body shuddering she silently blinked, "Yes, Mistress".

Slip Up

By Karen Godson

"Come here girl", she heard through the sides of her very tightly fitting leather hood.

With ears completely covered, girl could never be certain whether Mistress was speaking *to* her or *about* her. It was not polite to eavesdrop; nor was it allowed that she disobey a direct order to "Come here".

she crept forward, off of her comfy pet bed, dragging the shackles behind her that held her steadfast to the table leg across the room from Mistress' chair. she dared not make a peep, but kept her head down and made her way to Mistress' feet. Once there, she lowered her shoulders to the floor, ass in the air, legs apart as she was taught to do. She waited for her signal to rise to all fours. The wait was excruciating. Knowing that the punishment for approaching Mistress without being summoned was being banished from Mistress' presence, she trembled and prayed that she had heard correctly.

Then came the pat on the head, followed by a hand grasping her chin and raising it upward. Still not yet allowed to open her eyes, girl kept them squeezed tightly shut. She felt the hand on her chin release, and she knew it was then permitted that she open her eyes.

"Mistress?" she whispered cautiously. "May I serve You Your tea?"

Mistress sat back in Her high wing-backed Ox Blood leather reading chair, and put Her feet up. As they hovered above girl's back, it was obvious that the answer was "No tea".

girl crawled a few inches closer to her Goddess, her ankles straining against the metal shackles, and lowered her chin again. There she stayed as the beautiful black stiletto boots came to rest on her back. The cool leather and the even colder steel heels made her catch her breath and jump just a little. It was not little enough though, and the second she felt herself do it, she regretted being so weak.

Mistress has always said, "Furniture does not move on its own". girl broke a very important rule, to never disturb Mistress' relaxation time. Now Mistress' feet had slipped and were not longer where She had placed them on girl's naked flesh.

Mistress let out an exacerbated sigh, and dug Her heels into girl's skin. "Was I not clear enough for you?" She grated. "Did you not understand My instruction?"

Horrified at the thought of Mistress' disapproval, girl wanted to disappear into the floor boards. she swallowed hard.

"Mistress was very clear. girl made a grievous mistake and accepts full punishment, Mistress."

As soon as she said the word "punishment" her pussy went into spasm. Oooh, the thought of Mistress's flogger lacing its stripes across her naked cheeks was just too much to bear. The anticipation of those scrumptious welts gave girl's already wet lips a sudden flood of lubrication.

"Please Mistress," she begged. "girl means only to serve You and please You." Too little too late, though, she thought. What's coming is my own doing, and i welcome the burn.

Mistress bid girl stand up, and told her to go to the armoire and fetch the Flogger. Of course, girl stood up immediately and shuffled, still shackled, over to the cabinet where all the implements of pain and pleasure were housed. she carefully removed the Flogger; a perfect device hand-made by Mistress, with nine leather strips each ending in a delightful welt-inducing knot. girl practically came the second she touched the cool leather, but knew better than to orgasm before Mistress had given her permission. Come to think of it, she was not permitted to orgasm until Mistress had dealt the pre-determined number of blows, and then laid the Flogger down. Greater and far less pleasurable punishment came if girl accidentally came too soon. Some of Mistress' tools were for good pain, and some were for bad pain. girl had sense enough to know the difference, and thanked her lucky stars that the Flogger was the chosen mode of correction this time.

Back at the feet of her Mistress, girl placed the Flogger in Her hands, and again lowered her face and shoulders to the floor. This time, her ass was to be held as high as she could get it. her legs were to be spread as far apart as the shackles would allow, and her hands were to remain under her head. she was forbidden to move a muscle as the Flogger bit into her flesh, one, two, three, ten times. With the last blow came the tears; but these were tears of joy.

"Thank You, Mistress", was spoken after each lashing, and in the end, the tenth "Thank You" signaled the completion of her punishment. she was ordered to put the Flogger back in its place, and return to her position as Mistress' footstool. This was an honor that Mistress had not chosen for any of Her others, and for this girl was eternally grateful. With ankles burning, knees throbbing and her ass singed, girl proudly stayed still as an ottoman until Mistress sent her back to her blanket for the night.

"Tonight, I will make My own tea. And you will try harder tomorrow" Mistress said as she turned out the light and left the room.

girl sighed, her ass still smarting, and fell happily to sleep in her chains.

Glossary

1950s household: a relationship which follows the dynamic of the male bread-winner role and female home maker, meal preparer and child raiser. In female Dominated households, the male would be kept at home while the Woman took over the traditional bread-winner role.

24/7: a relationship in which the partners are in their roles as Dominant and submissive, or Mistress and slave, at all times, in all environments.

69: a sexual position in which partners lie head to toe while giving each other simultaneous oral pleasure.

A

Age Play: a role play scenario in which one partner assumes the role of parent and one of child. This is NOT necessarily linked to pedophilia, but rather can be a form of expressing the Nurturer/nurtured aspects of the relationship.

Anal Beads: a strand of plastic or glass beads that may be uniform in size or gradually smaller to larger. These beads are meant to be inserted into the anus or vagina, in order to provide stimulation. May be used in Orgasm Control Training.

Androgyny: the lack of typical appearance for one's assigned sex, making them appear to be either of the opposite or indeterminate sex.

Ass Play: anything to do with anal sex or anal stimulation, with or without penetration.

B

BDSM: An acronym for Bondage, Dominance, submission (or Sadism), Masochism.

Ball Gag: a ball, usually made of rubber or other flexible material, that fits snugly into the mouth to prevent speaking, eating and drinking. The ball is attached to a head strap that prevents it from being removed without the use of hands.

Ball Stretching: the practice of tying or binding the testicles and scrotum, and applying weights to create downward pressure. Used in CBT and Body Modification.

Bare Bottom Spanking: the act of spanking a submissive's or slaves bare buttocks, usually with an open hand or wooden paddle.

Bastinado: erotic foot torture, such as the slapping of the soles of a person's feet with a hard wooden spoon.

Bathroom Use Control : a Dominant's control over the bodily functions of Her slave or submissive.

Begging: the act of pleading, usually on one's knees, in front of a Dominant.

Behavior Modification: a science which uses techniques of positive and negative reinforcement to create or prevent a desired behaviour.

Belting: the using of a leather belt or strap to inflict a spanking.

Biting: using teeth to cause slight to moderate pain when closed on the flesh of the receiver.

Blindfolds: covers that fit snugly over the eyes to prevent the wearer from being able to see anything.

Body Worship : the act of a slave or submissive bathing, moisturizing, caressing, massaging and giving sexual attention to his Dominant's body as if She were a Goddess.

Bondage: the state of lacking freedom, whether it is physical or mental confinement.

Boot Worship : the act of cleaning, kissing, caressing and sometimes licking the boots of a Dominant.

Bound: tied or restrained, commonly by the wrists and ankles.

Bullwhip: a long whip usually made of leather, with a hard handle and tassel at the end of the whip. This whip is capable of making a loud cracking sound when used in the right way by snapping it in the air sharply at the end of the stroke. Originally used to startle cattle and move them forward without risk of injury to the ranchers.

Butt Plug: usually made of rubber, silicone or latex, a butt plug is a cone shaped object with a flat base and indented neck. The Butt Plug is inserted into the anus and held in place when the anal sphincter closes over the narrow neck. Used in anal play, training and punishment.

C

Cage: a metal box with bars, that locks from the outside. A slave or submissive may be locked in a cage for any length of time, as determined by their Dominant.

Cat o' Nine Tails : a medium length whip with a hard handle and nine individual strands or leather or similar material, usually ending in knots.

CBT: "Cock and Ball Torture" involves bondage, physical pain and sometimes piercing of the male genitalia.

Chastity: denial (either self imposed or dictated by a Dominant) of any sexual gratification.

Chastity Device: locking "cage-like" apparatus that fits over male or female genitals, and which allows for urination but no sexual stimulation. The device is usually locked on by the Dominant and She holds the key, ensuring that the sub or slave can not masturbate or have sex with anyone else while She is not present.

Cinching: the severe tightening of a corset to cause the "wasp waist" shape. Used in Forced Dressing and Body Modification.

Collar: a piece of jewelry, usually leather or metal, that is locked around a slave's neck indicating that it is owned by a Master or Mistress.

Collar and Lead /Leash: a collar worn around the neck of a slave and attached to a leash which is held by the slave's Owner. This is to ensure that he cannot go far from Her sight.

Confinement: being kept in a closed space without the ability to let one's self out.

Control: to decide and determine the fate of Oneself or another.

Corner Time : a form of negative reinforcement in which the offender stands facing the corner of a room, and is forbidden to turn around, or change position until released by the Dominant. Often this is combined with Speech Restriction and/or Eye Contact Restriction.

Corset: an article of clothing usually made of satin or silk material, with evenly spaced rigid bones or ribs inside that serve to constrict a person's waist when criss-crossed laces on the back are tightened. See Cinching.

Crop: a short wand shaped tool, wrapped in woven fabric or leather, and usually with a leather loop on the end. The crop is used to spank an offending slave or for play sessions between Sadists and Masochists.

Cross Dressing: the act of wearing clothes that are typically worn by people of the opposite sex.

Cuckold: a male submissive partner who is forced to watch his female Dominant partner have sex with other men or women.

Cuffs: a type of restraints worn around the ankles and wrists.

Cunnilingus: the act of giving oral stimulation to a woman's genitals.

D

Depilation/Shaving: the removal of body and facial hair through shaving with a razor, laser, electrolysis, plucking, waxing, sugaring or other applied topical solutions.

Dildo: often, but not always a phallic shaped hand-held apparatus that is used during sex for internal stimulation, either vaginal or anal. Note: a dildo does not vibrate. For battery powered toys, see Vibrators.

Discipline: a punishment that is meted out in order to correct an unwanted behaviour.

Domestic Servit ude: the voluntary undertaking of housekeeping and other domestic chores by a submissive, for a Dominant. This can be considered another type of BDSM relationship, where there may or may not be sexual or intimate relations between parties. In some cases it is strictly a service arrangement.

Dominance: the rule, superiority and control of one person over another.

Double Penetration:

- Meaning 1- the use of two "toys" on one person. One object, usually a dildo or vibrator is inserted into the anus and the other into the vagina
- Meaning 2- penetration involving two women who share a double-ended dildo at the same time
- Meaning 3- the act of one man having anal intercourse with a woman while another man's penis penetrates her vaginally

D/s: an acronym for Dominance and submission, Dom/sub or Domme/sub.

Dungeon: a place where medieval play or torture scenes occur. Many people in the BDSM world create a play space in their basement or spare bedroom, although it may or may not resemble a dungeon.

E

Electrical play : the use of a static electric wand (called a Violet Wand) applied to the receiver's skin, to illicit a response from the small zap that it delivers.

Encasement/Entombment: the total confinement of a person by means of surrounding them in a substance that allows for zero movement. Some such substances may involve dirt, such as in a Live Burial fantasy, or plaster to create a full body cast.

Erotic hypnosis: the use of mind control to illicit a sexual response, or engage in erotic activities or fantasies.

Exhibitionist: a person who becomes aroused upon knowing that other people are seeing him or her in intimate situations, such as undressing or having sex.

Eye Contact Restriction: a rule that forbids a slave or submissive from looking his Dominant in the eye, until told to do so.

F

Face Slapping : open handed slapping of another person's cheek. There are safe and unsafe ways to slap a face, and these are best researched on the many BDSM sites online. Face slapping should be done only by an experienced Dominant as a slap can cause painful injury to the jaw, eyes or nose if poorly placed.

Female ejaculation: the release of large amounts of clear vaginal fluid with orgasm, usually after prolonged G-Spot stimulation.

Fingernails: a perfect tool for leaving marks that last only a few days.

Fire Play: the use of a flammable substance wiped on the skin of the receiver, then lit on fire and very quickly extinguished. Fire play is a hard limit for many in the Lifestyle.

Fisting: the act of one person inserting a fist and sometimes forearm into the vagina or anus of another person.

Flogger: a hand held device, usually made of leather or suede but sometimes other material such as nylon rope. Used to inflict pain for either pleasure or punishment.

Forced Dressing: the ordering of a Dominant to Her submissive, to wear clothes of the opposite sex. Sometimes used in Humiliation or punishment, but also may be used in play.

Foot Massage: the rubbing and manipulating of the feet of another, for the purposes of relieving pain or relaxing the muscles of the feet.

Foot Worship : the act of massaging, washing, moisturizing and giving a pedicure to the feet of a Dominant. Sometimes involves sole licking and/or toe sucking.

G

Gender Play : the reversal of genders in a relationship, either temporarily or permanently. A male would dress and act as completely female and a woman would dress and act as completely male.

Gimp: an objectified slave that has had its arms bound to its sides, and its leg movement restricted, a gag of some sort to restrict speech, and a tray or other article of service attached to it so that it may serve tea or drinks like a robot. NOTE: Gimps do not have a gender. They are objects or possessions to be employed into their Owner's service.

H

Handcuffs: metal restraints that lock around the wrists and that are joined together by a very short but string chain.

High Heels: shoes with heels that are elevated, causing the wearer to walk predominantly on their toes.

High Protocol: a set of strict rules and guidelines within the BDSM and D/s worlds that set a standard for the way submissives and slaves should speak to Dominants, and to each other.

Hood: a form-fitting leather (or other material) covering that is worn over the entire head, sometimes complete with blindfold, ear muffs and a ball gag for sensory deprivation. Some hoods can be locked when zipped or tied so that only the key holder can remove them from the wearer.

Human Furniture: tables, chairs, stools, benches, lamps and other household objects that are created when a slave poses in a certain position. Some tables may have a top placed on them so the Owner and Her friends can put their drinks down and play cards while the slave continues to pose perfectly motionless for hours.

Humiliation: using degrading, insulting and demoralizing phrases to lower the self esteem of another person. In most cases, the slave or submissive has asked the Dominant to humiliate them, because it is something they desire or need to make them happy.

K

Kneeling: the act of getting down on one's knees in front of a Dominant, for the purposes of honouring Her, submitting or pleading.

L

Latex: a substance that is used to make Fetish clothing, such as gloves, nurse uniforms, tightly fitting dresses and mini skirts. Latex fans may go as far as to have entire head-to-toe suits made of latex that can be done up to render them immobile. Latex Fetishists are aroused sexually by the smell, sight or feel of latex.

Leather: cow hide that has been treated to make it soft and able to be made into clothing. Jackets, harnesses, masks, restraints and even dungeon furniture are often made of high quality leather. Some Dominants like to dress in all black leather outfits, including boots and gloves. Leather fetishists are people who derive sexual arousal from the smell, sight or feel of leather.

Leaving Marks: the deliberate scratching, welting or bruising of a person from caning, whipping, open hand spanking, flogging or other means of corporal punishment or intense physical play.

M

Male Submission: the giving over of power from a submissive male to his dominant Partner of any gender.

Masks: face coverings that do not envelop the whole head. A mask may or may not have a gag and/or blindfold attached.

Masochist: one who derives pleasure from pain (not the same thing as a slave or submissive).

Master: the male Owner of a human voluntary slave.
Masturbation: the act of touching oneself for sexual pleasure, using one's own hands or other objects to bring about sexual release through orgasm.

Mind Control: the use of suggestive and subliminal methods such as hypnosis to illicit changes in the behaviour or thoughts of another person.

Mistress: the female Owner of a human voluntary slave.

Mistress/slave or M/s: a relationship between a voluntary slave of any gender and the slave's female Owner.

Mutual Masturbation: the act of two or more partners pleasuring themselves at the same time, as they watch each other but do not touch each other.

N

Needle Play: the use of a surgical needle to puncture the skin of the receiver, sometimes in ornate patterns. Needle play is a hard limit for many in the Lifestyle.

O

Obedience Tr aining: the use of positive reinforcement or punishment to modify a slave's or submissive's behaviour. See also Behaviour Modification.

Oral S ervice: the act of giving oral pleasure aka cunnilingus to a dominant Woman. See also "Queening". While oral service does not necessarily involve confinement, Queening always does.

OTK: an acronym for Over The Knee, meaning a position in which the slave or submissive lies over the Dominant's lap, bare bottom up, and receives open hand or paddle spankings as a form of discipline.

P

Paddling: the act of spanking or beating a submissive's behind with a (usually) wooden paddle for the purpose of discipline or play.

Pain: the feeling of physical discomfort when nerve endings are super-stimulated.

Piercing: the act of inserting a sterile needle through a person's flesh, then replacing the needle with a piece of permanent jewelry.

Pinching: the act of squeezing another person's skin between your thumb and forefingers, with enough force to cause mild to severe pain.

Polyamory: the practice and belief in loving more than one partner at a time, in a consensual and committed relationship.

Power Exchange: See TPE aka Total Power Exchange.

Protocol: a set of rules and guidelines that are considered to standardize the behaviours of a group or culture. The main rule in BDSM is to keep all activities "***Safe, Sane and Consensual***".

Pussy Worship : the act of a submissive person kissing, washing, orally servicing and otherwise paying personal attention to their female Dominant's genitalia.

Q

Queening: the act of a slave or submissive giving oral pleasure to a Dominant Woman while his head is held inside an enclosed stool that She sits on. The stool consists of four solid sides, one having a hole cut out through which the submissive's neck fits. Once the head is inside, this "door" is locked shut, and the submissive or slave is held in place as long as the Domme is seated on the stool.

R

Restraints: any form of wrist or ankle cuffs, harness, spreader bars or other article which, when locked onto the restrained, prevents them leaving the spot where they are bound. To be in full restraint is to be completely immobilized.

Rimming: the act of orally stimulating the outer area of the anus.

S

Sadist: a person who derives pleasure, sometimes sexual, from inflicting pain on another person. NOTE: In BDSM this means a **consenting** person aka Masochist (see "Protocol").

Safe Word : a word that is discussed between activity partners before engaging in BDSM play. The word is spoken by the submissive to indicate that he or she has reached the edge of their comfort zone, and wishes to go no further. Depending on the Master or Mistress in question, a slave may not be allowed to have a safe word. After all, a slave has given up all rights.

s.a.m.: a "smart ass masochist" is a submissive who derives some kind of pleasure from breaking rules, mouthing back to his/her Dominant and generally being a trouble maker. The unruly behaviour is exhibited for the purposes of soliciting punishment, because the s.a.m. derives pleasure from pain.

Sensory Deprivation: the forced removal of all outside stimuli. This involves the use if ear plugs, nose plugs, blindfolds, hand restraints and gloves (to take away the ability to reach out and feel things). Sometimes the slave or submissive will be placed in a small dark room with no windows, in order to assure that no sound or light gets in.

Service-oriented submission: the desire of certain submissives to perform various chores, errands and tasks for the purposes of alleviating the work load of a Dominant, not necessarily within a relationship. Some submissives wish to do things for a Dominant for the sole purpose of knowing that they have been of help.

Shaving: the removal of facial, cranial or body hair by means of a razor. Some Dommes require their male submissives to be clean shaven all over.

Shibari: the Japanese art of tying intricate knots for the purpose of restraining the wearer. Originally used in war time by Japanese soldiers for torture and confinement of prisoners, this rope work has now become a fine art practiced by BDSM Lifestylers all over the world.

slave: a person who has given up all rights in his or her own life to a Dominant. Once "collared" (found under C in this Glossary), the slave refers to the Owner as Mistress or Master.

Spanking: the act of a Dominant using an open hand to slap a slave's or submissive's bare bottom for the purposes of disciplining.

Speech Restriction: a rule which forbids a slave or submissive from speaking or uttering a sound, until given permission by his or her Dominant.

St. Andrew's Cross : a wooden structure built in the shape of a large standing "X". A slave or submissive is restrained at the wrists and ankles with arms and legs spread apart, while standing for the purposes of whipping or other corporal punishment. It may also be used as furniture for some sexual play.

Strap-on: a typically penis-shaped rubber, latex or silicone toy that is fitted into a metal ring on the front of a special harness and worn in the front of the pelvic bone just like a real penis. The strap on is used for lesbian sex, or for times when a Dominant may want to penetrate the submissive.

Submissive (n oun): a person who identifies as submissive in nature, wishing to follow rather than lead, and to defer to others for decision-making. Submissive people often seek out service rolls such as housekeeper, chauffeur, personal assistant or beauty consultant.

Switch: a person who may feel and behave dominantly with one partner, yet be submissive with another. This term may also refer to people who sometimes take a dominant role, and other times a submissive role, within the same relationship.

T

Teacher/student: a role play scenario in which the Dominant partner plays the role of school teacher, and the submissive assumes the role of pupil. Often this involves OTK Spanking, Caning and Corner Time. See Glossary for descriptions of these terms.

Toys: any item or object that can be used in play. Examples are dildos, Violet Wand, needles, fire sticks, paddles, floggers, restraints and nipple clamps.

TPE aka Total P ower Ex change: the act of giving over complete control of one's life to Another.

Transvestism: the practice of wearing clothes that are typically worn by people of the opposite gender Trans=cross and Vest=clothing.

Tribute: a financial gift given to a Dominant by a submissive or slave, as a way of honouring Him or Her. Some wannabe Dominants ask for financial tribute or gifts before They will even meet a submissive in person, but most are genuinely looking for a partner. The latter do not ask for tribute, but rather demand a submissive's time and service.

U

Urethral Sounding : The act of placing a catheter into someone's urethrea, and then pumping air or liquid in and listening through a stethoscope to the sunds this makes inside the person's body

V

Vanilla: the term given to any person or activity that is not within the realms of Dominance and submission, or BDSM. Commonly, but not necessarily accurately also referred to as "Normal".

Vibrators: battery operated wands, often shaped like a penis, that vibrate when turned on. Some have more than one speed, and some have clitoral or anal stimulators attached.

Violet Wand : a device that delivers a static shock or zap to the receiver. Used in play and punishment applications.

Voluntary Slavery: the act of giving over complete ownership of one's mind, body and emotional being to someone in a position of authority. This decision is not to be taken lightly, as it is intended to be life-long and irreversible by the slave once the Contract of Voluntary Servitude is signed by both the slave and the Master/Mistress.

Voyeurism: the practice of watching other people undressing or engaging in intimate activities.

W

Wartenberg Pinwheel : a nickel-sized spiked metal wheel with a wooden or plastic handle, used by doctors to determine nerve sensitivity in patients. The wheel, when rolled across bare skin, especially tender areas, can bring about a strong pain/pleasure response.

Water S ports: activities which involve contact with urine. Also known sometimes as a Golden Shower.

Wax Pl ay: the act of heating wax and dripping it on a slave or submissive, often on the nipples and genitals, in order to illicit a pain/pleasure response. Research is required before playing with hot wax of the first time, as burns may result in improper use of the wax.

Whip: a long strand of leather or synthetic material that ends in a knot or small tassel, and has a hard bat-like handle

Resources:

Collarme.com : an online community and dating site for those in the BDSMM community, or those who are interested in learning more about the Lifestyle

Fetlife.com : a social community of Fetishists and BDSM, D/s , S/M and M/s enthusiasts. Fetlife is the "Facebook" of the Kink world!

About the Author

From early in her childhood, Karen Godson has had a strong will to be right, and to be in charge. She admits that she loves to be noticed, and still fondly remembers winning a place in the Peel Region School Board's Poetry Anthology at the age of eight, with her poem called "The Runaway".

Karen now works as a "pen for hire", while continuing to write poetry and other short stories, both kinky and "Vanilla". She chooses to write under her real name, declaring, "If I'm not proud enough to stand behind my work, then maybe it isn't worth publishing."